Big R_____
the Big Wash

Written by Jill Eggleton
Illustrated by Sandra Cammell

Big Red came to stay
with us.
"He's dirty," said Mum.
"We'll have to wash him."

2

"He won't like having
a wash," I said.

3

Mum got the shampoo.
"You can put this on him,"
she said.

I put **all** the shampoo
on Big Red.

He had bubbles all over him.
Then he ran off . . .
out the gate.

Mum and I ran after him.
"Come back!" I called.
But he didn't.

Big Red went into a garage.
He jumped onto a truck.
Then . . . the truck went
into the car wash!

The man in the garage
came out.
"Big Red is in the car wash,"
said Mum.
"We must get him out."

"We won't get him out now,"
said the garage man.
"He'll be OK.
He'll get a good wash."

9

Mum and I looked
in the car wash.
We could see Big Red.

We could see the water
going **swish**, *swash* . . .
all over him.

"Big Red must like
the car wash," I said.

The car wash stopped.
The truck came out
with Big Red still on the back.

Big Red jumped
off the truck.

He licked us with his big, wet tongue.

"You are clean," I said. "You won't have to be washed for a year."

Big Red sneezed all over Mum.
"You can go in the car wash,"
said the garage man.

But Mum said,
"**No thank you!**"

Signs

Guide Notes

Title: Big Red and the Big Wash
Stage: Early (4) – Green

Genre: Fiction
Approach: Guided Reading
Processes: Thinking Critically, Exploring Language, Processing Information
Written and Visual Focus: Signs, Speech Bubbles, Thought Bubbles
Word Count: 227

THINKING CRITICALLY
(sample questions)
- What do you think this story could be about? Look at the title and discuss.
- Look at the cover. What do you think Big Red could have been doing to get so dirty?
- Look at pages 2 and 3. Why do you think Big Red wouldn't like having a wash?
- Look at pages 4 and 5. Why do you think Big Red ran out the gate?
- Look at pages 8 and 9. How do you think Mum and the boy feel about Big Red in the car wash?
- Look at pages 12 and 13. How do you know Big Red is happy to be out of the car wash?
- Look at page 14. Why do you think Mum didn't want to go into the car wash?

EXPLORING LANGUAGE

Terminology
Title, cover, illustrations, author, illustrator

Vocabulary
Interest words: dirty, car wash, garage, sneezed, shampoo, bubbles, tongue, truck
High-frequency words: him, called, must, could, still, won't
Positional words: on, over, out, into, onto, in, off
Compound words: onto, into

Print Conventions
Capital letter for sentence beginnings and names (**B**ig **R**ed, **M**um), full stops, commas, exclamation marks, quotation marks, ellipsis